BUSINESS IS WAR

9 Classic Rules of War for Winning Big in Business

 NATIONAL INSTITUTE OF BUSINESS MANAGEMENT

SPECIAL REPORT N282A

AUTHOR
Morey Stettner

EDITOR
Kathy A. Shipp

EDITORIAL DIRECTOR
Annette Licitra

PUBLISHER
Philip W. Clark

© 1998, 2001, National Institute of Business Management, 1750 Old Meadow Road, Suite 302, McLean, VA 22102-4315. Phone: (800) 762-4924. All rights reserved. No part of this book may be reproduced in any form or by any means without written permission from the publisher. Printed in U.S.A.

ISBN 1-880024-15-2

"This publication is designed to provide accurate and authoritative information in regard to the subject matter covered. It is sold with the understanding that the publisher is not engaged in rendering legal, accounting or other professional service. If legal advice or other expert assistance is required, the services of a competent professional person should be sought."—*From a Declaration of Principles jointly adopted by a committee of the American Bar Association and a committee of publishers and associations.*

BUSINESS IS WAR

9 Classic Rules of War for Winning Big in Business

CONTENTS

Introduction: Business Is War 1

1. Overview: The 9 Principles of War 5

2. Objective 9

3. Offensive 13

4. Mass 17

5. Economy of Force 23

6. Maneuver 27

7. Unity of Command 33

8. Security 37

9. Surprise 43

10. Simplicity 47

Appendix 53

INTRODUCTION

Business Is War

War is a matter of vital importance to the state, the province of life or death; the road to survival or ruin. It is mandatory that it be thoroughly studied.

—Sun-Tzu, *The Art of War*

Learn to think like a general

Countless books advise serious career advancers to think like a CEO. But that leaves a crucial question unanswered: "How do CEOs really think?"

In this Special Report we'll introduce you to a way of thinking that can turbo-charge your career. Our source: successful military generals who have triumphantly led their troops into battle throughout history.

Every leader is unique, yet there's a remarkable similarity between how corporate chieftains and top generals think. Senior executives may not even realize it, but they frequently adopt war principles to lead their companies into a more profitable future.

In fact, military thinking pervades corporate America. Companies routinely declare "war" on competitors. Their leaders often speak in battlefield metaphors of a "full frontal attack," "defending our turf" and even "penetrating enemy lines." They describe the competition as "the walking wounded" or simply "the enemy."

Take the three big consumer electronics companies that are immersed in a catfight over dueling formats for new digital video disc (DVD) recorders. Leaders of the three rivals—Panasonic, Pioneer Corp. and Philips Electronics NV—expect a hard-fought battle over who gets to dominate the DVD market. At the 2001 Consumer Electronics Show in Las Vegas, the companies jockeyed for position in advance of their new product rollouts by firing salvos at each other with warlike aggression.

When Komatsu, a heavy equipment manufacturer, wanted to increase its market share, its president adopted a rallying cry that every employee took to heart: "Encircle Caterpillar." Or, when Hugh L. McColl, former CEO of Bank of America Corp., began acquiring banks in Florida in 1981, the ex-Marine dubbed the campaign "Operation Overlord" after the Normandy invasion during World War II.

Similarly, the imagery of war often carries over into politics. Witness the 2000 presidential election. Two days after Al Gore retracted his concession to George W. Bush and challenged Florida's election results, a top Republican strategist said, "They have started a war here . . . full political and legal nuclear war." Then, when a Florida circuit judge ruled against Gore's request for a manual recount of 13,000 disputed votes in south Florida, a Bush ally declared, "If this was the Second World War, we just crossed the Rhine."

At first glance, it may seem strange to compare the gritty, bloody tragedy of war to the relative safety of business or political contests, but there are many similarities between how military, corporate and political leaders operate. Some examples:

■ **They all focus on the big picture.** The very nature of war requires the general to embrace the entire sweep of events. For example, a Marine Corps officer managing an amphibious assault must consider the use of sea power, jet fighters and bombers, tanks, helicopters, ground troops, artillery, paratroops and dozens of other instruments of force. Same goes for the fast-charging manager, who must think in broad terms to weigh the cost and benefit of decisions, the interplay between one division's strategy and another unit's efforts, the ever-changing actions of employees, contractors and customers, and the larger forces that shape the marketplace, such as technological advances and Federal Reserve policy.

■ **They also must rely on teams.** The traditional rigidity of military hierarchies does not negate the importance of teamwork among soldiers. Individuals collaborate in countless ways to prepare for war, execute their battle plans successfully and sacrifice personal glory for the greater good of the unit. Similarly, employees at all levels are expected to function in groups. Team-building seminars emphasize the need for sharing information, unclogging communication channels and finding ways to build on one another's ideas to produce better results.

In this age of employee empowerment, distributing authority among teams is one of the most popular ways for CEOs to motivate their workers and foster collaboration. In fact, one of today's most popular business books is Gary Hamel's *Leading the Revolution* (Harvard Business School Press, 2000) in which the author rallies readers to forge alliances to produce bold results. He suggests that readers should think of themselves as "revolutionaries."

Business leaders who have served in the military oftentimes transfer their teamwork training to the workplace. Case in point: Neil Caggiano, who runs a successful New York-based flower business. Caggiano said in *MyBusiness* magazine (Nov./Dec. 2000), "I was in the Marines for three years. They taught everyone to work with each other and that you don't let each other down. It's teamwork, and that's what I try to instill."

■ **Effective leaders rely on trust.** A military commander must establish trust; otherwise, his troops might hesitate to follow orders in the heat of battle. A manager who fails to earn his employees' trust faces a similar danger. Talented individuals may quit or resort to "malicious compliance" when they have reason to suspect the words, motives and actions of their boss.

Military strategists have distilled nine principles of war that transcend time and culture. Among the strategists who contributed to this development were the Chinese sage Sun-Tzu in the fourth century B.C., the Prussian general Karl von Clausewitz in the 19th century and Alfred Mahon, an American, in the 20th century.

Hannibal Barca, the lead general of Carthage (now Tunisia), embodied many of those nine principles when he attacked Rome—marching 90,000 men, 12,000 cavalry and more than 30 elephants across North Africa, Spain and the Swiss Alps. From 218 to 203 B.C., as he slashed away at the early Roman Empire, he proved to be one of the first "modern" war thinkers. His tactics were so successful that his sworn enemy, Rome, wound up copying his methodology to counterattack him!

The U.S. Army formally adopted the nine principles of warfare in 1921. Since then, those principles have guided the commanders of America's fighting forces, helping them make strategic decisions, lead their troops and respond to aggression.

Significantly, the better business schools recognize the value of the nine principles of war for business leaders and include them in their M.B.A. curricula. But the corporate landscape is littered with examples of businesses that failed to follow the principles, only to suffer severe setbacks.

For example, Sears did not fight off Wal-Mart, and today Wal-Mart is the dominant force in the retail industry. Bill Gates, Microsoft's chairman, misplayed his hand in a historic antitrust case and alienated the judge with his inflexibility and arrogance. Chrysler's 1998 merger with Germany's Daimler-Benz has backfired; the two companies' leaders haven't been able to mend their cultural rifts and work together to gain market share. (In the third quarter of 2000, Daimler-Chrysler reported a loss of $512 million, compared to a $1 billion operating profit the previous year.)

Whether you're managing a staff of hundreds, running your own small business or advancing your fast-track career strategy, your success largely hinges on your ability to solve problems, communicate persuasively and plan and execute your objectives effectively. By thinking like a great general and using the nine principles that follow, you'll have the tools you need to become an unstoppable force.

1. Overview: The 9 Principles of War

From the battlefield to the boardroom

A general knows that to win a war, you need to learn how the enemy thinks. Only then can you map out how to advance your position strategically without walking into a firing line.

But waging a successful battle requires more than knowing your adversary. You must also apply certain tools to ensure that your attack achieves its stated purpose. That's where the nine principles of war kick in.

As you review these concepts, which have been drummed into thousands of military men and women at all levels, you may notice that a common theme resurfaces: Leadership, whether on the battlefield or in the boardroom, flows from the judicious exercise of power. The following principles offer a "reality check" to help any general—or any fast-track business leader—ensure that his actions are rooted in sensible beliefs and proven strategies that lead to victory.

1. OBJECTIVE
Direct all efforts toward a clearly defined, decisive, obtainable goal.
Perhaps you've already heard that "unless you know where you're going, you won't know when you arrive there." Military campaigns revolve around carefully articulated objectives (often referred to as "missions"). For example, whenever a U.S. president considers going to war, he must first speak to the nation and explain his goals in a concise, persuasive manner. Otherwise, the public (and Congress) may not support the use of force.

It's not enough to say, "Our goal is to annihilate the enemy." You need to be specific and articulate the actual gains you expect to attain. A general who directs everyone's attention to an overriding objective can motivate the troops more effectively and keep them focused on the primary task.

2. OFFENSIVE

Seize the initiative in a decisive manner, retain it and exploit it to accomplish your objective.

Brilliant military strategists understand the need to charge an enemy at the right time—not wait around and play defense. This "seize, retain and exploit the initiative" mentality assures that fighting units think in terms of exerting force rather than merely withstanding attack. By going on the offensive, you take direct steps to influence the outcome of a battle—to shape your destiny instead of allowing others to pummel you into submission.

3. MASS

Concentrate your combat power at the decisive place and time.

Every general wants to enter the battlefield with an overwhelming advantage in combat power, with the outcome of the battle never in doubt. Although that goal is not always achievable, generals bring as many of their resources to bear as they possibly can. Successful generals properly train, rest, equip and position their forces before engaging the enemy so as to deliver the most powerful blow from the outset.

4. ECONOMY OF FORCE

Allocate minimum essential combat power to secondary efforts.

Every available resource must contribute directly to achieving the main objective. Secondary objectives are not allowed to take on a life of their own. By directing their forces squarely at their No. 1 objective, successful generals generate sufficient mass to win the war.

5. MANEUVER

Place the enemy in a disadvantageous position through the flexible use of combat power.

Successful generals maintain flexibility in their plans and their forces so they can outmaneuver their opponents and exploit opportunities that may develop as the battle unfolds. For example, a general may use the element of maneuver to go quickly around a major concentration of the enemy force and cut off supply lines in the rear, thus weakening the enemy before the direct assault begins. Or, he might attack an enemy line in a different place than planned because recent intelligence had shown unexpectedly weak defenses there. In the Persian Gulf War, for example, NATO forces staged a "Hail Mary" run around Iraqi troops to cut off their supply lines and prevent their retreat.

6. UNITY OF COMMAND

For every objective, there should be unity of effort under one responsible commander.

Successful missions can have only one commander. That commander may delegate large amounts of authority to competent subordinates but can never delegate responsibility. That way, every individual involved knows clearly who is ultimately in charge of the operation and who will make the most difficult calls. Unity of command minimizes confusion and dissension among the troops and increases the speed and effectiveness of decision making.

7. SECURITY

Never permit the enemy to acquire an unexpected advantage.

The highest responsibility of any general is to protect his troops—to minimize casualties and ensure that his force remains intact to fight another day. Offensively, this means maintaining secrecy about your plans and deceiving the enemy regarding his intentions and abilities. Defensively, this means retaining enough forces in reserve to guard against counterattacks and sabotage.

8. SURPRISE

Pounce on the enemy at a time or place and in a manner for which he's unprepared.

Catching an enemy off guard is the easiest and fastest way to achieve the objective with the least casualties. The enemy is likely to be terrified, confused and unable to react in a concerted fashion.

9. SIMPLICITY

Prepare clear, easy-to-understand plans and clear, concise orders to ensure thorough understanding.

The best military plan is the simplest one that will accomplish the mission. Simplicity will reduce the risk of error in execution because all those involved will better understand the significance of their roles and take the right action.

2. Objective

If a man does not know to what port he is steering, no wind is favorable.

—Seneca (4 B.C.–A.D. 65)

Direct all efforts toward a clearly defined, decisive, obtainable goal

Everett Alvarez Jr. spent eight and a half years as a prisoner of war in Vietnam—the first 18 months in solitary confinement. He was beaten, tortured and fed dead birds and sewer-water soup.

Alvarez, who was the first American pilot shot down over North Vietnam, knew his objective: Stay alive.

Today, Alvarez runs a thriving management consulting firm, Conwal Inc., which he founded in 1988. Based in McLean, Va., the company has 200 employees and annual revenue of more than $15 million. Alvarez applies the lessons of his wartime experience to operating his business. He sets specific goals and lets nothing stand in his way of attaining them.

Like any successful business owner, Alvarez has a business plan to guide his company's growth and plot his strategy. Unlike many executives, however, he sticks with his plan through thick and thin. For instance, when

Eastman Kodak Co. offered to make his firm a distributor of a floppy disk for government use, Alvarez declined because it wasn't part of his original plan.

"Everett won't do stuff that's outside the mission," says Kevin Riley, Alvarez's business partner.

Alvarez understands the first principle of war: Declare an objective, and direct everyone's focus on achieving it. Cut through all the clutter to uncover what really matters, and reinforce that crystal-clear message so that everyone knows exactly what they're striving to accomplish.

Identifying the objective may sound obvious, but many managers overlook this basic task. They may figure it "goes without saying," so they never bother to articulate their objectives. What's more, they often resist the practice of writing down what they want; this leads to inconsistency and confusion during execution.

The result: a ready-fire-aim mentality in which they fail to accomplish their objectives. They don't progress in a disciplined, incremental fashion toward a larger goal.

What's worse, some would-be career advancers prefer not to hone in on just one objective. They'd rather pursue two or three ends at once. But with only a vague, fuzzy sense of what they're after, they wind up wasting valuable time going around in circles.

When James L. Barksdale arrived in Silicon Valley to run Netscape in January 1995, he inherited 100 employees—many of them bright engineers and driven managers—who were pursuing dozens of diverse goals. He knew the organizational chaos had to end, so he directed everyone's focus on one objective: to make Netscape the fastest-growing software company ever (Lotus Development Corp. was the company to beat).

"Jim views his mission in life as boiling everything down to a few basic principles that motivate people," says Craig McCaw, who was Barksdale's boss at McCaw Cellular.

A company that identifies and communicates a key objective can boost its standing, its stock price and market share. For example, Advanced

Micro Devices has fought for years to overtake industry leader Intel, the dominant maker of chips for personal computers. The relentless underdog, AMD persevered and maintained its focus despite myriad obstacles. Today, AMD's new Athlon processor is slightly faster than Intel's most advanced Pentium III chip. As a result, the Athlon is forcing Intel to lower prices on its comparable chips to stay competitive. That in turn gives AMD inroads into winning new business. For the year 2000, AMD's sales increased 63 percent over 1999 to a record $4.64 billion.

Another example: Stanley Furniture Co. in Stanleytown, Va., which fills customers' orders in three weeks or less (compared to the average delivery time of about eight weeks). Its responsive service flows from its efficient production runs and statistical process controls, which all focus on a central objective: to cut costs and improve service by bypassing pricey distributors and selling directly to retailers through agents or sales representatives.

As any seasoned military leader will tell you, the secret to setting an objective isn't just deciding what matters most. You also have to stick to it, despite the inevitable roadblocks and crises that erupt. With proper planning, those obstacles can be anticipated in advance and will not discourage or distract you from achieving your objective.

Of course, circumstances can change: Key personnel might sustain injury, unexpected opportunities may open up or enemy incursions may jeopardize continued pursuit of a key objective. In such cases, it may be necessary to rethink or even revamp an objective, but it's essential to do so only after careful consideration of all key factors.

Too often, however, changes in objectives result when weak leaders simply treat their objectives as a matter of convenience, modifying them or completely changing course based on "the crisis of the day" or unanticipated difficulties.

"I find it's best to arrive at an objective during a time of calm and stability," said Carl A. Modecki, a widely respected turnaround specialist who has helped five large Washington, D.C.-based organizations bounce back from years of poor performance. "I'm a strong believer in conducting strategic planning that in turn produces clear objectives. At one company I ran, I set new objectives every two years with the input of the executive committee and an outside facilitator. That let us reflect on where we were going as an organization on a regular basis, when there was no crisis to interfere. You don't want to hash out an objective only when your whole company is under fire."

Like many leaders, Modecki finds that one of the benefits of directing employees' attention to a clearly defined objective is that it helps everyone know with certainty what they're trying to accomplish. When a CEO drills home an undeniably powerful objective, every worker gains a sense of mission. There is no dispute over whose job matters most and no need to divine an organization's future from obscure political battles. "A clear objective puts everything out in the open," he says.

"There was a time when I was plotting our company's quarterly results, and the numbers just weren't hitting the goals I had previously announced," Modecki recalls. "This went on for a few more quarters, where we kept coming up 3 or 5 percent short. I was disappointed, but even though we weren't meeting the objective, I insisted that we stick to our game plan. Other executives wanted to lower our sights, but I fought them hard. If you keep communicating why an objective exists, what it means and why you're not about to change midstream, then eventually people will believe in it."

✔ Executive Checklist

1. Does my plan have one clear objective that, if met, will achieve the success I seek?
2. Is the objective attainable?
3. What conditions would trigger a re-evaluation of the objective?
4. Can I get "buy-in" for the objective from all necessary resources?

3. Offensive

In war, the only sure defense is offense.

—Gen. George S. Patton

Seize the initiative in a decisive manner, retain it and exploit it to accomplish your objective

For 31 years Rod Walsh has owned Blue Chip Inventory Service in Sherman Oaks, Calif. A former Marine and Vietnam veteran, Walsh has applied his battlefield experience to building a successful company in a low-glamour but ruthlessly competitive field.

In 1998, he faced one of his biggest challenges. "Every Marine learns not to stand by idly and watch events take shape that could overwhelm him," Walsh says. "On June 26, the second- and third-largest inventory service companies in the U.S. became one. Rather than wait to be put on the defensive—or wait for someone else to fill the vacuum—I decided to attack."

For Walsh, taking the offensive involved two steps. First, he analyzed his larger competitor's weaknesses. There were four areas he could exploit:

1. Many of the customers of this new mega-inventory service had previously chosen to work with one service over the other. Now, in effect, they had to work with a service not of their own choosing.

2. Most large customers in this business, not wanting to put all their eggs in one basket, prefer to work with multiple vendors.

3. Many of the customers of the newly merged company might fear changes in pricing, personnel or procedures.

4. Many of these customers might feel they were being held captive by the loss of competition.

Second, Walsh acted with lightning speed, instructing his staff to make sales calls to more than 2,000 of the competitor's customers. To compete in far-flung geographical areas, he quickly arranged alliances with other inventory services across the country to accept new business.

Seizing the offensive—or being "proactive," as management consultants like to say—is often a high-risk gamble. Fast-track managers may want to nab a string of promotions by leading their organization to new heights, but launching a bold first strike can result in a highly visible blunder if it backfires. What's more, retaining the initiative over time and fully exploiting it require shrewd planning and tactical skill.

When you go on the offensive:

■ **Recognize an influential event.** Beware of clinging to the status quo in the face of upheaval in your industry. Study competitors' actions with a clear head, free of bias, prejudgment or preoccupation, which can cloud your ability to think. By calmly analyzing an enemy's strategy, you can separate the decoys and diversions from a big, potentially threatening push against you.

■ **Act now.** Don't let your competitors' aggressive moves immobilize you. When you learn of major news that affects your business, dig for details immediately. Don't wait for a convenient moment to investigate. Time will work against you if you delay.

■ **Rally your forces.** You must motivate your employees to join you in a gutsy, offensive campaign. If they're riddled with fear or doubt, they won't execute their assignments in the proper frame of mind. Help them appreciate the magnitude of the situation, and instill pride so that they will want to conquer the competition.

Aelred J. Kurtenbach is CEO of Daktronics Inc., a $100 million company that makes computer-controlled scoreboards, time and temperature signs and schedule board displays at airports. He co-founded the firm in 1968 and has built Daktronics into a market leader in large-screen video scoreboards.

Kurtenbach loves to seize the initiative and beat rivals to new sources of profit. In 1997, for example, when the company had annual earnings of 18 cents a share, Daktronics started making custom giant-screen video scoreboards for sports stadiums. Just three years after entering this line of business, Kurtenbach's company had nabbed about half of this profitable market. Its annual earnings rose to 68 cents a share in 2000.

Given the speed with which high-tech "new economy" companies either grow or die, it's especially important for them to play strong offense. Monster.com, the leading job-listing site on the Internet, has maintained its advantage in large part by airing bold, in-your-face TV commercials during the Super Bowl.

In recent years Monster.com has invested heavily in these high-profile ads. During the 2001 Super Bowl telecast, for instance, the company unveiled four new commercials as part of a planned $200 million marketing push.

The Casualties

The corporate battlefield is strewn with the remains of companies that failed to take the offensive and paid the price. This often occurs when a leader does not treat new competition seriously or simply pretends it does not pose a threat.

If you don't seize the initiative, you can lose your competitive edge while others take risky but smart steps to advance their position.

Jeffrey Taylor, Monster.com's founder and CEO, knows he's at war with rivals such as Hotjobs.com, so he ups the ante every year with innovative TV commercials that reinforce the company's brand in a memorable way. Rather than react to competitors' commercials, he seeks to dominate them on the advertising battlefield and keep them in Monster's shadow.

Taking the offensive rarely comes easily. It demands vigilance and vision. But when you decide to charge enemy lines, you give yourself the chance to score a resounding triumph. If you just stand your ground, you never give yourself a chance to win.

✔ Executive Checklist

1. Is my plan basically offensive in nature, seizing the initiative to control the fate of my career and my company's profitability?
2. What internal strengths or external weaknesses can I exploit by taking the offensive?
3. Exactly what offensive actions will I take?
4. How will the offensive actions I propose support my objective?
5. Do I have sufficient resources available to take these offensive actions?
6. Can I afford *not* to take offensive action?

4. Mass

Don't bunt. Aim out of the ballpark.

—David Ogilvy (1911–1999), ad man turned guru

Concentrate your combat power at the decisive place and time

In the early 1990s, Corning Inc. had weathered a series of storms. Profits at the big Corning, N.Y.-based glass and technology company were down, affiliate companies had suffered severe losses, and protracted litigation diverted management's attention from ongoing operations.

Roger Ackerman, Corning's chairman and CEO, knew he had to restructure the organization to get it back on track. But he also realized he didn't have all the answers on how to proceed, so Ackerman formed a committee called "Corning Competes." Its role: to propose ideas to help the company regain its footing and devise long-term success strategies.

Ackerman selected a group of bright, creative employees at all levels and assigned them to this initiative. He needed to ensure that they could give 100 percent to "Corning Competes" rather than treat it as an adjunct to their regular jobs.

He made a decision that shocked everyone involved—he assigned the group to work on the project full time.

"Here was a CEO who took dozens of really talented contributors out of their normal positions for a long time—about six months," says Quinn Spitzer, chairman and CEO of Kepner-Tregoe, a management consulting and training firm in Princeton, N.J. "This group included several vice presidents and other people with critical jobs throughout the company. Ackerman sent a message that he wanted them to concentrate fully on 'Corning Competes' without any distractions."

A manager's ability to channel an organization's "combat forces" (whether in the form of brainpower or sheer brawn) at the appropriate time and place to produce maximum results is what military leaders refer to as "mass." By not spreading yourself too thin, you can hit two or three priorities hard, rather than making an often futile stab at tackling 10 or 20 at once.

Boston Chicken's management failed to learn this lesson. It grew successfully in the early 1990s by providing "home-replacement meals," such as rotisserie chicken and meat loaf for the dinner crowd. But in 1996 it attempted to lure lunch customers by launching a line of carved meat sandwiches and kids' meals with giveaway toys. The restaurant chain never won over enough lunch diners because it couldn't manage such a complex menu—and it alienated its base of dinner customers in the process. By 1998 the company was facing a severe cash crunch.

By contrast, when Pepsi Bottling Group Inc. launched Sierra Mist, a new lemon-lime soft drink, it concentrated all its resources on making the new product an instant smash. On a single Saturday in October 2000, the company loaded every single truck with Sierra Mist. All 10,000 routes were devoted to stocking the new beverage in stores. By Sunday, Pepsi had achieved national distribution of its new drink.

Earlier that same month, all 20,000 of Pepsi's salespeople had flooded retailers with point-of-sale displays and free samples. *Investor's Business Daily* (Feb. 26, 2001) compared Pepsi's successful product launch to a "wartime invasion."

Applying the principle of mass depends on your ability to spot an opportunity. Take Lennar Corp., a Miami-based home builder with a great track record of "bottom fishing." The company gobbles up land during economic downturns. "The company's strategy is to wait for the right moment to step into downtrodden markets and snap up competitors—and their land holdings—at discount rates," according to *Investor's Business Daily* (Dec. 27, 2000). Thanks to Lennar's land purchases in Texas and California during the real estate slumps of the early and mid-1990s, the company has racked up 31 percent annual earnings growth over the past five years.

Whether you're running a worldwide business or managing your team, directing all your firepower where it will have the most impact is a valuable skill. It takes a high degree of discipline and self-awareness to unleash your energy where it matters most.

"When there's business that I want to win, I need to dedicate all my resources, such as time, attention and people, to the account," says Craig Roberts, president of Capital Real Estate Partners, a Cincinnati-based real estate brokerage firm. "You have to see it as a prize that's waiting to be won."

For Roberts and other successful executives, applying the principle of mass to business leadership involves more than allocating sufficient resources to get the job done. It's also necessary to assemble the right mix of resources so that you can attack the enemy at full strength. Ideally, you want to recognize the range of tools at your disposal and put them to best use.

Consider how Kmart Corp. signed up 1 million subscribers to its Web site, BlueLight.com, in the first 14 weeks after its launch. Kmart publicized its Web presence with mass mailings to millions of its regular customers. It also gave away 4 million sign-up compact discs in its stores. While rivals such as Wal-Mart and J.C. Penney tweak and redesign their Web sites, Kmart continues to gain subscribers.

In recent years, management consultants have used the term "core competencies" to describe the skills or traits that top performers must embody to contribute most successfully to a productive organization. When a manager understands each of her employees' core competencies, she can focus everyone's effort on what they do best. As managers evaluate their workers' core competencies, they are applying the principle of mass to invest their best assets to fix a problem or capitalize on an opportunity.

Brent Filson, a former Marine infantry officer who's written four books and built a busy management consulting practice in Williamstown, Mass., credits the principle of mass with helping him build his enterprise from the ground up. "I've found that mass is critical to success in waging any battle, whether in war or in business," he says. "In the military, it's called concentrating your essential combat power on a mission. In the business world, I call it producing results. My experience has taught me that it's absolutely necessary to put all my energy and all my resources into getting the results I set out for myself and my company."

Filson, who teaches sales training workshops, emphasizes this theme when coaching professional salespeople to increase their production. He has created a report card that lists all the reminders salespeople need to keep in mind, and in his seminar he assesses individuals' performance based on how well they exhibit their most impressive traits.

Consider the case of a life insurance agent who tends to get nervous during sales presentations. Her parents' untimely death years ago left her family in dire financial straits. As a result, she strongly believes in the value of buying life insurance—a belief that finds natural expression when she talks about her products with friends. She needs to bring that same emotional intensity to her "moments of truth" (i.e., when she's trying to win over a new client). Otherwise, she will lose the chance to persuade people to buy.

"When they're really concentrating on their strengths and playing up what they do well, then they use mass to their advantage," Filson concludes.

One example of how success comes to organizations that capitalize fully on their strengths is the growth of Gatorade as a thirst-quenching beverage. At the end of 2000, PepsiCo Inc. and Coca-Cola Co. fought to buy Gatorade's parent, the Quaker Oats Co. Pepsi won the prize in a $13.4 billion deal. Both cola giants coveted Gatorade because its brand managers plow 30 cents of every dollar back into marketing. Michael Jordan splashes it on his forehead in TV ads, and athletes in every major sport drink it on the sidelines—in paper cups adorned with the brand logo. Thanks to Gatorade's brilliant marketing, its sales have risen from $100 million to $1.8 billion over the last 15 years.

Gatorade's marketing savvy underlies a significant lesson in the use of mass: Money talks. Making a concentrated financial investment to dislodge the enemy can work wonders. By spending huge amounts of cash in a systematic manner, you can pummel adversaries into submission.

Witness the 2000 elections, when U.S. pharmaceutical companies contributed heavily to Republican campaigns. *The Wall Street Journal* called it "the biggest and costliest corporate campaign in U.S. political history, spending more than $80 million to keep the Democrats from regaining control of Congress." Their investment paid off.

On a personal level, you can test to what extent you amass your power and unleash it at the proper time and place. How? Think about how you manage your time. Step back and evaluate whether you're working on the most critical issues facing your organization. Are you immersing yourself in what matters most (or the activity that promises the biggest payoff)? Or do you try to fight too many battles on too many fronts all at once?

✔ Executive Checklist

1. What is the minimum level of resources required to achieve my objective?
2. Will my plan direct the maximum resources available at the time and place that will have the greatest impact on achieving my objective?
3. Am I making the best use of each resource at my disposal?

5. Economy of Force

It's easy to decide what you're going to do. The hard thing is figuring out what you're not going to do.

—Michael Dell, founder of Dell Computers

Allocate minimum essential combat power to secondary efforts

You can spot an organization that fails to apply economy of force by two telltale characteristics: soaring expenses and high overhead costs. Take the financial services industry, where some companies invest millions of dollars in opulent offices housed in gleaming towers with splendid views of the city skyline. Some CEOs spend exorbitant amounts of their company's money to purchase expensive artwork to adorn their office walls.

What these companies fail to realize is that many customers value thrift over ostentation. That's why a cost-conscious mutual fund giant such as the Vanguard Group proudly informs its customers (who are also shareholders) that its corporate offices in Valley Forge, Pa., are not fancy palaces filled with plush carpeting, million-dollar paintings and executive chefs who serve filet mignon every day to the top brass. Rather, Vanguard Group operates from plain, even drab, surroundings where managers make due with used desks and pass-along chairs.

The same goes for Cisco Systems Inc., the world's No. 1 maker of Internet gear and the most successful stock of the 1990s. Every executive in Cisco's San Jose, Calif., headquarters has a 10-by-12-foot office. No one has a window view. No one has an extra fancy chair; managers all sit in blue and gray standard-issue chairs like those in the conference rooms.

But reducing costs isn't the end of the story. A successful leader—or organization—makes every dollar count. Spending becomes a means of producing the most "bang for the buck." The purpose of economy of force is to reserve as many resources for the main battle effort ("mass") as possible. Thus, every use of resources must be considered in terms of its contribution to the organization's main objective—its mission or its bottom line.

"The way that I make sure we don't get bogged down in secondary goals is that I don't set secondary goals," says Ray Zeek, CEO of JD Steel Co., a Phoenix-based commercial construction firm with about 350 employees. "I don't believe there should ever be secondary goals. I've always operated my business with the philosophy that if you can't do it right, then don't do it at all. If I see my people getting distracted by projects that don't really matter, then I set them straight."

Zeek gives an example of how economy of force played a vital role in a long and exhausting battle. "My firm was one of many construction teams that worked on the Boston Harbor cleanup a few years ago," he recalls. "It was a massive, complex project that required all of our effort just to keep up. I had a few people who just didn't throw themselves fully into this deal. They were off doing far less important things that didn't translate into much revenue for us. When I found out, I explained that they weren't helping the company by neglecting to put all their talent and energy into our primary effort at the time: Boston Harbor."

Some secondary objectives are fine, however, as long as they support your primary goal. But that means every employee must understand how these ancillary projects will clearly help the organization pursue its larger objective.

Of course, many managers don't set out to create bloated overhead structures. More typically, a division manager might assemble talented teams to solve short-term problems, but the groups can linger long after they have served their purpose. Such teams often sustain themselves with "busywork," hiring consultants and more staffers to justify their continued existence.

Many executives find that as their firms grow, it's hard to prevent internal bureaucracies from sprouting. As a result, employees waste time and resources fighting yesterday's battles—or each other—rather than preparing to confront tomorrow's challenges. Success can become your enemy if it leads to unnecessary appendages, which add to costs and dilute management attention.

At Cisco Systems, fast growth had created some inefficiencies. For example, Cisco lacked an effective financial reporting system when its current chief financial officer, Larry Carter, came aboard in 1995. Carter quickly realized that his employees were wasting time on ancillary tasks instead of reporting the firm's sales, margins and discounts on a daily basis.

The solution? Carter prodded his team to abandon minor projects and devise a central database of financial information. Armed with Web-based financial software and a new commitment to giving Cisco managers the latest financial results in real time, the company can now track sales better and make more accurate financial projections to Wall Street.

Another example: Morrison Knudsen, a once-dominant commercial construction firm that built Hoover Dam. Based in Boise, Idaho, the company fizzled in the early 1990s when its controversial CEO at the time, William Agee, spent more time running ancillary businesses (such as its rail car and locomotive operations) than its core construction and engineering activities.

Even great leaders can squander their resources by taking their eye off the ball. Howard Schultz, the respected chairman of Starbucks Corp., redirected some of his management's efforts to Internet investments in 2000. Executives paid less attention to the company's core business—coffee retailing. The result? Starbucks took a $58.8 million pretax charge in its fiscal fourth quarter of 2000 to cover its abortive Internet investments.

From a personal standpoint, applying economy of force means reserving the majority of your work hours to address your primary efforts. During the less productive hours of the day (say, after 6 p.m.), you may want to contemplate only those secondary efforts that you truly care about.

By not wasting time on insignificant matters, you maintain perspective. It's hard to lose sight of your priorities if you steadily pump most of your energy into what matters most.

✔ Executive Checklist

1. Are all secondary objectives clearly focused on supporting the primary objective?
2. Are minimum resources devoted to the secondary objectives?

6. Maneuver

To achieve victory, we must as far as possible make the enemy blind and deaf by sealing his eyes and ears, and drive his commanders to distraction by creating confusion in their minds.

—Mao Tse-tung (1893–1976)

Place the enemy in a disadvantageous position through the flexible use of combat power

Millions of Americans who were watching the ABC network on the night of April 30, 2000, suddenly lost their television picture. Then a printed message flashed across the blue screen: "Disney has taken ABC away from you."

Time Warner Inc., owner of the cable systems that bring ABC to viewers, had decided to take ABC off the air after abortive negotiations with Disney Co. (ABC's owner) over the cost and terms of including certain channels in its cable packages. Disney's president, Robert Iger, likened Time Warner's move to kill ABC's signal to launching a "tactical nuclear weapon." Yet all-out war had already broken out between the two media giants.

Just seven weeks before, Disney had outmaneuvered Time Warner in Houston after Time Warner had switched the Disney Channel from its basic to premium service. Disney's executives swarmed into Houston and ran full-page ads in the local newspaper, scaring people into thinking Time Warner might take away ABC next. Disney further stung its adversary by announcing a satellite-giveaway program in which TV viewers could get Disney-subsidized installation of satellite dishes if they left Time Warner for a competing service.

After Time Warner unplugged ABC on April 30, Disney resorted to equally shrewd maneuvering. It rallied public opinion against Time Warner for operating like an "arrogant . . . monopoly" and persuaded politicians and federal regulators to act against Time Warner's bully tactics.

The result? Time Warner sheepishly put ABC back on the air the next day and negotiated desperately to mollify Disney. The final agreement gave Disney almost everything it sought in a deal it estimated was worth almost $3 billion.

Disney's creative, flexible response to a potential disaster provides a vivid example of the importance of maneuver. By shifting gears quickly, finding a way to undercut competitors' positions and making the necessary resources available to make it happen, a shrewd CEO can land a body blow to even the mightiest foe.

One leader who is a master of maneuver is Roger Enrico, the longtime chairman and CEO of PepsiCo. In March 2000, he stole a sizable share of teenage soda drinkers away from Coca-Cola by forming a marketing alliance with Yahoo, the big Web-navigation company that's popular among teens. While Coke dabbled in Internet marketing, Pepsi swept in and arranged with Yahoo to promote its sodas and sell its merchandise online. Pepsi drinkers could also collect points to redeem for video games and other prizes on Yahoo's Web site.

Another leader who has outmaneuvered competitors is Kenneth Lay, CEO of Enron Corp., the world's leading integrated electricity and natural gas company. The big Houston-based company ranked No. 1 in innovation among 431 companies in a 1997 *Fortune* magazine survey of corporate reputations. Clearly, Enron's innovations are paying off: Its shares rose 87 percent in 2000, outpacing a 54 percent gain in Standard & Poor's utilities index.

In the 1980s, Lay noticed that other natural gas companies were trying to stand their ground in a tightly regulated market. He could have played it safe and done the same. Instead, he boldly rowed Enron upstream into unregulated businesses, directing his firm's force in an entirely different direction.

"We thought there'd be more opportunity here to differentiate ourselves on products and services and make a profit at it," Lay told *Fortune*. "Many other companies felt they needed to stay in the regulated pipeline business just to survive."

Lay's company also built three new power plants in 1999. Although cheaper than most modern plants, they were also much less efficient. Rivals questioned Enron's dubious investment, but Lay planned to fire up those plants only when electricity prices surpassed a certain level—a move that made their operation profitable.

Lay's efforts expose an underlying truth of flexible maneuvering: The only way you can capitalize on your competitor's weakest link is to understand your competitor's situation. By stepping into its shoes and appreciating both its biases and its challenges, you can attack from a position of strength. That's how many superior generals have defeated larger, more heavily equipped adversaries.

The first step to maneuver properly, whether you're running a corporation or plotting your career path, is to perceive a problem accurately. This involves acknowledging an opportunity in fair, accurate terms before you act on it. The military calls this information "military intelligence." It gives generals the information they need to maneuver effectively.

This same approach works in the corporate battlefield. Every workday morning, top officials at Southern New England Telephone Co. (SNET) in New Haven, Conn., convene in the "war room" to monitor every newspaper and television advertisement in Connecticut (where it sells local, long-distance and cable TV services). SNET hires a service to track ads because it wants to know right away if any of its competitors in the telephone industry has launched a campaign that will lure away customers.

Daniel Miglio, SNET's former CEO, began a "24-hour rule" by which SNET has 24 hours to deliver a competitive response to any new gimmick or announcement by a rival to win business. By keeping a vigilant watch over its competitors' moves and making flexibility a priority, SNET can maneuver quickly and stay ahead of the curve.

Careful planning often helps. During the 1992 presidential campaign, for instance, Bill Clinton's "war room" consisted of a group of political advisers who could mobilize quickly when the elder George Bush and his aides leveled attacks or accusations. Clinton's team prepared fact sheets in advance that addressed what they anticipated would be criticisms from the Bush camp. As a result, whenever Bush lashed out, the media almost instantaneously received concise faxes that summarized Clinton's response. The press coverage wound up presenting both sides, thus undermining Bush's numerous attempts to "get something negative to stick to Clinton."

To maneuver successfully, you must sometimes improvise as events unfold. You must prepare your organization to have the flexibility, creativity and communication necessary to change direction quickly and smoothly. Your employees must be skilled at analyzing data, identifying all options and drawing valid conclusions. You want to attract employees who can size up a situation quickly and exhibit poise while demonstrating a fearless, problem-solving mentality.

In the early 1970s, for example, Datsun's American marketers were facing a highly competitive marketplace and trying to distinguish Datsuns (now Nissans) from all the competitors' sports cars. When Datsun shipped three boatloads of mustard-yellow B210s with tan interiors from its factory in Japan, its marketers feared that the cars were too ugly to appeal to Americans. They decided to add a black stripe to the side and stick a bee decal on the trunk. The so-called Honeybee became a huge fad, especially in California.

To take a more recent example, consider how America's largest supermarket chain, Kroger Co., has fought off online grocery rivals such as

Peapod Inc. With its huge stores and high overhead, Kroger can't possibly compete with the convenience offered by Web-based delivery services. Instead, on its Web site it has offered coupons that customers can request by mail and then redeem when they shop at Kroger.

Of course, some attempts at maneuvering can backfire. When McDonald's launched a massive promotion to sell Big Macs and Egg McMuffins for 55 cents each in 1997, it wanted to woo diners away from Burger King and other rivals. But instead of putting its competitors at a disadvantage, McDonald's hurt itself by cheapening its brand and cannibalizing sales of its profitable Extra Value Meals.

Flexibility comes with preparation. By anticipating how your business might change and plotting possible ways to maneuver, you can stay on top of any upheavals in your industry. That's smarter than standing by and watching events unfold around you. Identify your options now so that you can act quickly later.

✔ Executive Checklist

1. Can I gather sufficient information about the competition to guide maneuvering?
2. Have I selected and organized resources with enough flexibility to change direction quickly and smoothly based on new information?
3. Are my people and I innovative enough to find and exploit competitor weaknesses as they appear?
4. Have I anticipated and planned for likely competitor responses?

7. Unity of Command

Surround yourself with the best people you can find, delegate authority and don't interfere.

—Ronald Reagan

For every objective, there should be unity of effort under one responsible commander

The U.S. military follows a strict chain of command. In every skirmish in every war, a supreme commander takes full responsibility for leading his troops into battle. The soldiers accept such leadership and fall into line, heeding orders from above with fanfare. It is this principle of unity of command that enables large organizations to pull together and produce greater results than individuals could achieve on their own.

In business, there can be only one boss on every assignment. The chain of command is a tool used to attain an objective and direct the efforts of far-flung employees. At the same time, however, the wise leader doesn't hog the spotlight or look down on workers as mindless drones or mere order-takers.

Take Jim Mann, CEO of SunGard Data Systems Inc., a software firm with annual sales that exceed $1 billion. Mann, a former Air Force pilot, joined SunGard in 1983 when its sales were less than $50 million a year.

While he takes responsibility for the company's overall performance, he doesn't micromanage. Instead, he has created dozens of individual business units that operate as profit centers with their own management.

"One positive thing I learned in the Air Force was the virtue of an organization where responsibility is fixed at each area," Mann says. As the company has grown, he's introduced new layers of management and given autonomy to "group executives" who control their own business units.

Unity of command requires leaders to delegate authority while maintaining ultimate responsibility. They are like stewards guiding their people to victory. But in so doing, they loosen the reins so that others can take charge and "step up" to deliver results.

Dennis Gillings, founder and CEO of Quintiles Transnational Corp., the world's largest contract drug-testing company, understands the need for unity of command. Over a 16-year period, Gillings transformed a start-up firm with 10 employees into a global powerhouse with 11,000 employees in 27 countries. He led the charge while placing trust in his workers—who in turn prospered as a result.

"If you don't give people authority, you won't get the best people," Gillings told *Investor's Business Daily* (July 14, 1998). "They'll move on. If they stay and you never give them authority, you're fooling yourself that they're the best people."

Establishing unity of command might sound simple, but it's a rule that is often violated. In many cases, senior managers don't want to play favorites or offend a manager's peers by putting him or her in charge of a project. Such splitting of command responsibilities can ease some immediate discomfort but at the risk of the mission's failure.

For example, British companies frequently grapple with unity-of-command issues because the chairman and CEO are almost always a different person (unlike in U.S. companies, where one leader can and often does hold both titles).

Take the case of British Airways. Lord King, the chairman, worked alongside Colin Marshall, the CEO. Both possessed strong personalities and ran the airline during a difficult stretch when a flurry of major decisions that would greatly affect the company's future had to be made.

The atmosphere in the executive suite was ripe for dissension. But Marshall took charge with his forceful, articulate personality. King realized there had to be one responsible commander calling the shots, so he gave Marshall the space to act. They disagreed in private on certain strategic moves, but as far as the rank-and-file were concerned, Marshall was their boss.

U.S. companies can face similar breakdowns in unity of command. At Toys "R" Us Inc., Michael Goldstein agreed to turn over his duties as CEO to Robert Nakasone in 1998. Goldstein became chairman and promised to give Nakasone the freedom to run the company without interference. But during Nakasone's early months as CEO, Goldstein sat next to him at weekly management meetings. At one point, Nakasone lashed out at the company's new president, Bruce Krysiak, for a mistake. Goldstein later questioned Nakasone's outburst, arguing it wasn't warranted. Nakasone wound up resigning as CEO after 18 months, in part due to conflicts with Goldstein.

When commanders jockey for position and the hierarchy grows fuzzy, organizations tend to falter. Effective leadership in the military sense requires the talent and willingness to make a final decision and expect full compliance.

When a CEO divvies up responsibility for a single objective among two or more top lieutenants, problems are likely to result. That's because it creates a fragmented reporting system, which can yield confusion and contention. Under the principle of unity of command, a leader gives one individual the responsibility to run projects and lead campaigns. There is no ambiguity among employees as to who is ultimately in charge.

During William J. Bratton's remarkable two-year stint as New York City police commissioner in the early 1990s, crime fell 38 percent. Bratton credits his success to his ability to maintain responsibility while putting highly effective lieutenants in charge of specific projects.

"The New York police commissioner is a very powerful person, and the structures of the NYPD reinforced that power," he told *Fortune* (Jan. 13, 1997). "All decisions flowed from the top, all requests flowed from the top. I consciously sought to give away a lot of that power, while holding those to whom I gave it very accountable."

As in Bratton's case, the best managers lead without dictating policies or bossing others around. They do not fancy themselves tyrants. They allow authority to cascade down an organization, but they never relinquish their ultimate responsibility for steering their staff toward greater success.

Leaders delegate authority but never responsibility.

✔ Executive Checklist

1. Is only one person ultimately responsible for each mission I assign?
2. Is that individual informed and clearly up to the task?
3. Do all people taking part in the mission know who the single commander is and what their individual roles and authority will be?
4. Are effective two-way communications in place to pass information and directives in the heat of battle?

8. Security

It is an invariable axiom of war to secure your own flanks and rear and endeavor to turn those of your enemy.

—Frederick the Great

Never permit the enemy to acquire an unexpected advantage

A general's primary responsibilities are to protect his troops and ensure the survival of his forces to fight another day. Failure to meet those dual responsibilities is the fastest route to a court-martial.

There are both defensive and offensive elements to the principle of security. From a defensive standpoint, generals must disperse troops until the time of the attack to prevent their decimation in an air or missile attack, and must set up guard posts and patrols to protect perimeters from surprise attack or saboteurs. They must also keep some troops in reserve during assaults to cover their rear from counterattack.

Exposing their troops to harm isn't the only risk that commanders face. Preventing them from fighting back can turn loyal troops into disgruntled rebels. Consider the fiasco on the first day of the 1999 World Trade Organization meeting in Seattle. Law enforcement authorities failed to make it safe for delegates to thread their way through protesters to attend the opening ceremony, which had to be canceled. What's worse, police officers were ordered by their superiors not to defend themselves if pelted with bottles and rocks—and were told not to stop vandals from smashing store windows. Naturally, the police officers were upset and humiliated.

Similarly, managers must avoid tying the hands of their employees or stripping them of their ability to think independently. If workers feel that an adversary is gaining an unexpected advantage, their morale can plummet and they may lose confidence in their leadership.

At the same time, managers must avoid the temptation to put everything at risk in single-minded pursuit of their objectives. Never "bet the company" on any objective. Maintain sufficient resources in reserve to cope with unexpected events or provide for an orderly retreat that will let you fight another day.

As many specialty retailers struggle to stay afloat, Tiffany & Co. continues to show strong sales gains. One reason for its success: While it used to cater solely to the very rich, it has recently tried to woo upscale—but not wildly affluent—consumers. By shifting its customer base and offering gift items in the $100 to $500 range, it has increased sales at a healthy clip without sacrificing its exclusive image.

Moreover, Tiffany has defended itself against direct marketers by launching a successful Web site and catalog. It has also began manufacturing more jewelry on its own rather than buying it from outside suppliers.

On a more personal level, security plays an equally crucial role in an executive's success. For Richard Buckingham, president of GoalStar Business Strategies Inc., a Bethesda, Md.-based management consulting firm, maintaining security helps him build his client base.

Buckingham learned about the principle of security while taking a Civil War seminar at the Gettysburg battlefield. He said Gen. George Sears Greene "spent the whole morning of July 2 having his men dig 4- to 5-foot dirt walls to protect a hill. He ordered his men to chop down trees and stack mud for many hours in 90-degree heat—and they were in wool uniforms! So you can imagine how much they grumbled at first about having to do that. But sure enough, when his regiment got attacked at 4 p.m. that day, the protective wall helped Greene and his men fend off 5,000 to 6,000 guys charging at them with guns and cannons."

When asked to reflect on the lesson he learned from Gen. Greene's leadership, Buckingham emphasized the need to think ahead and plan for your security. In his case, that means nurturing the long-term prosperity of his consulting business—even if he must give up short-term gains in the process.

"It's important to have a security strategy, a long-term plan to protect yourself against the competition," he says. "One way I do that may seem counterintuitive: I refer clients to my competitors on occasion if I think they'll benefit. Sure, I may lose short-term business, but I'm building a more secure, long-term relationship with them. By establishing trust, I'm giving myself and my business more security."

Offensively, generals maintain secrecy regarding planned operations or engage in active "disinformation" to make sure the enemy doesn't gain knowledge of their operations, which could endanger the success of their missions.

Building a buffer to protect yourself from competitors can pay all sorts of dividends. It's one of the primary reasons that McDonald's paid $173.5 million for the Boston Chicken chain (Boston Markets) in late 1999. McDonald's doesn't want to go into the chicken business, but it does want to prevent rivals such as Burger King and Wendy's from nabbing prime real estate in urban and suburban locations to open new outlets.

Look at the numbers: Opening a new McDonald's averages nearly $1 million, mostly for real estate and construction. Thanks to its purchase of more than 800 Boston Market restaurants, McDonald's will pay only about $230,000 plus conversion costs to spread its empire and block rivals from expanding.

At Amgen, a biotech company that has unveiled several blockbuster drugs, it's important to invest in cutting-edge medical research. But Gordon Binder, Amgen's former CEO, didn't just pour a lot of his company's profits into independent research. Instead, he formed collaborative arrangements with about 200 colleges and universities. That way, he gained exclusive rights to some of the nation's most esteemed researchers while shutting out his competitors. Amgen gained security by ensuring it got the "first look" at the findings of hundreds of brilliant scientists and research teams.

As another example, when James L. Barksdale, Netscape's former CEO, realized that computer hackers kept cracking his company's security code for its software, he decided to pay cash rewards to anyone who could find security flaws. Some managers argued that this was like paying a burglar to break into your home to test the alarm system, but Barksdale figured that he could gain security by providing incentives for others to quickly expose weaknesses in a controlled way.

Netscape's "Bugs Bounty" program helped the company uncover major flaws and correct them in a timely manner. Barksdale paid thousands of dollars to a host of hackers, but he viewed the money as a wise investment.

Another threat to security is the increase in industrial or economic espionage. Governments, too, are increasingly participating in such espionage in support of their national economic interests.

Now, more than ever before, it is important for managers to consider the need to protect sensitive information. Traditional protections include restricting access to those with a "need to know," data encryption and "compartmentalization" (i.e., splitting work on a project among different individuals or groups so that no one below the most senior level knows the entire plan).

Finally, it is important to have a contingency "Plan B" as an alternative to follow in case events don't turn out as expected. Having a Plan B and knowing when to move to it from Plan A can be critical to success. Ideally, Plan B may allow you to achieve your objective in spite of unexpected difficulties. At worst, it will help you make an orderly retreat with your resources intact to fight another day.

✔ Executive Checklist

1. What potential threats (for example, competitor counterattacks, shifts in marketplace demands, regulatory changes) do I need to defend against?
2. Have I devoted adequate resources to defending against those threats?
3. Have I protected sensitive information from competitor access through monitoring or espionage?
4. Is it useful to sow misinformation to deceive competitors about my real intentions?
5. Do I have a contingency or fallback plan to follow should my offensive not go as planned?

9. Surprise

Always mystify, mislead and surprise the enemy if possible.

—Stonewall Jackson (1824–1863)

Pounce on the enemy at a time or place and in a manner for which he's unprepared

A month after the Japanese attacked Pearl Harbor, the United States responded with a surprise of its own. Vice Adm. William F. Halsey, commander of the aircraft carrier USS Enterprise, penetrated deep into the Marshall Islands and launched 21 airstrikes against Japanese ships and planes, inflicting heavy damage.

"We did the exact opposite of what the enemy expected," Halsey wrote in his 1947 autobiography, *Admiral Halsey's Story*. "We did not keep our carriers behind the battle; we deliberately exposed them to shore-based planes."

The element of surprise works just as well in business. By foiling your competitors' expectations, you can shake their basic assumptions, drain their resources and undermine their confidence.

Sir Richard B. Sykes rocked the global pharmaceutical industry when he made a shocking announcement on Jan. 23, 1995. Sykes, the CEO of

GlaxoSmithKline, a British drug maker, revealed his intent to launch a $14 billion hostile-takeover bid for Wellcome, another British pharmaceutical giant.

This move surprised everyone for a number of reasons. First, British companies rarely resorted to hostile takeovers—a strategy that the proud Brits largely viewed as an unsavory, "American" mode of conducting business. Second, by the mid-1990s the merger boom had waned considerably in the pharmaceutical industry. With fewer big drug companies combining forces, the conventional wisdom was that the pressure had died down for large firms (like Glaxo) to "merge to survive." Finally, Sykes never telegraphed his move. Industry experts were genuinely shocked at news of the takeover bid; they didn't see it coming.

As a result of this bold move, Sykes avoided a protracted bidding war by nabbing Wellcome at a relatively low price. Better yet, he led Glaxo Wellcome to greater success by using his newfound might to compete more effectively and rush new drugs to market at a lower start-up cost.

Sykes then topped off the Glaxo/Wellcome merger with an even bigger move: combining Glaxo Wellcome with SmithKline Beecham in 2000. Through his deal making, Sykes offers a vivid example of an executive who applied the principle of surprise—the ability to "accomplish your purpose before the enemy can effectively react."

Tactical surprise does not necessarily result in the drop-jawed amazement of competitors. Even if a company expects to be attacked and prepares for the blow, an aggressor can still apply the principle of surprise by delivering a much more powerful punch than expected.

For example, in the early 1990s H.J. Heinz & Co. watched its pet food business erode. Its 9-Lives cat food, once a category killer, was turning into an also-ran. William Johnson, who in 1992 was president of Heinz's pet food products (he's now CEO of the parent company), surprised competitors and regained market share by resorting to "price-based costing."

In one fell swoop, he dramatically cut the price of pet food based on what consumers were willing to pay and drove the costs back from there (rather than the traditional approach of arriving at a price based on production cost plus retailer markup). After gathering research showing that most cat owners didn't want to pay more than 30 cents per 5.5-ounce can of 9-Lives (which had been selling for more than that), Johnson cut the price to just 25 cents.

The sudden upshot: Volume soared, revenues doubled, and earnings quadrupled at Heinz's pet food unit over the next four years. Other pet food companies were astounded at Heinz's bold price cuts and were ill prepared to respond to such an unexpected broadside.

On its own, of course, surprise does not guarantee success. The element of surprise is only as valuable as the way in which you follow through and capitalize on catching the enemy off guard.

"History gives numerous examples of commanders who, having surprised the enemy, failed to accomplish their strategic aim," writes Maj. Arthur L. Clark, U.S.M.C.R., an active member of the Marine reserves and a respected military historian, in *Warrior's Wisdom* (Perigee, 1997). "When contemplating a surprise attack, the commander must ask himself two questions: What is the opportunity I seek to create? What will I do if I succeed in creating this opportunity?"

Identifying the potential gains of staging a surprise attack can help you conduct a thorough cost-benefit analysis. If the risk is too great or the rewards too insignificant, then it will not make sense to strike a competitor at a time or place that's unexpected.

When John Bogle, the visionary architect of the Vanguard Group, rolled out the first index mutual fund in 1976 (allowing investors to "buy the market" at low fees), his competitors were totally taken aback. They weren't prepared to respond and sat on their hands while Bogle aggressively promoted his innovative brainchild. In fact, the other big mutual fund companies had been selling individual investors on the opposite of indexing—the benefit of having professional portfolio managers make their stock picks.

At first, Vanguard's competitors never seriously considered copying Bogle by launching their own index funds. They derided Vanguard's strategy and labeled the move "Bogle's folly." Now, of course, Bogle's move has proved a winner and Vanguard dominates the index fund market.

Some of the best strategic surprises are aimed not at subverting an enemy but at delighting a customer. By pleasantly exceeding buyers' expectations, a company can carve out a profitable niche.

For example, Morrison Management Specialists Inc. provides hospital food that's actually good. Granted, hospitals outsource their food services to Morrison primarily because the company can offer savings of 10 to 20 percent on food costs due to economies of scale. But Morrison delivers more than cheap institutional food. It prepares a varied menu for both patients and hospital staff, customizes its meals to accommodate patients with dietary restrictions and offers Pizza Hut and Subway products, so diners feast on great fare at reasonable prices.

Even if executives use surprise sparingly, they can intimidate competitors by keeping them guessing. The mere threat of catching an adversary asleep at the switch can work to your advantage. No one likes to be blindsided. If you create an atmosphere where your competitors never know what you'll do next, you can put them on the defensive while you charge ahead.

✔ Executive Checklist

1. What opportunities do I have to surprise my competitors in the time, place or strength of my offensive?
2. Can I realistically achieve the element of surprise?
3. If I'm successful at achieving surprise, what actions will I take to capitalize on it?

10. Simplicity

Remember, gentlemen, an order that can be misunderstood will be misunderstood.

—Helmuth von Moltke (1800–1891)

Prepare clear, easy-to-understand plans and clear, concise orders to ensure thorough understanding

As one of the few women to lead a Fortune 500 company during the past 20 years, Katharine Graham, head of the Washington Post Co., has fought many corporate battles. A hallmark of her leadership is her talent for communicating with her employees—ranging from arrogant, highly educated editors to rough-hewn pressmen working the graveyard shift.

The secret of her success? She thought before she spoke and made her remarks crisp and clear.

In her autobiography, *Personal History* (Vintage, 1997), Graham described how she sifted through the myriad issues of a strike by the pressmen's union to level with her staff about her decision to hire replacement workers. Rather than allow her points to get bogged down in complex discussions about contract terms and financial constraints, Graham said:

"Like the decisions made by each of you who continued to work in the strike, my decision was neither simple nor easy; and like your decisions it required me to weigh the claims of a variety of responsibilities. My conclusion is that I cannot in [good] conscience permit a situation to continue in which men and women in our trade unions, many of whom have worked here for many years, are faced with a bleak future because they must honor the picket lines of a group of men who are the highest-paid craft union workers in the building."

With that tidy summation, Graham enabled her listeners to understand her motives. To borrow newspaper lingo, she did not "bury the lede." Rather, she provided a simple statement upfront that captured the core truth of a vastly complicated dispute.

Just as generals know that they need to deliver clear, easy-to-understand orders to their troops, effective executives realize that the best-laid plans are only as good as the way in which they are presented to employees.

If a manager resorts to long or confusing explanations and then proceeds to give complicated or ambiguous directives, problems will usually result.

Whether you're a general or a team leader, ensuring simplicity requires taking three steps:

1. **Confirm that you have chosen** the simplest plan to accomplish your goal. Review your menu of options, and pick the one that strips away fluff and captures the nugget of what you're after. If you begin with a needlessly complicated plan of attack, the rest of your job grows more difficult as the odds of misunderstanding soar.

2. **Involve your employees** in the planning process, and be sure they can easily comprehend and execute your plan.

3. **Determine the best way** to communicate your plan. List all the vehicles at your disposal, then select the best one so that you present your message in unmistakably clear terms.

Tom McDonnell, president and CEO of U-Save Auto Rental of America Inc., understands the power of simplicity. His discount car-rental company competes aggressively with Enterprise Rent-A-Car, which has expanded across the country by opening new outlets at a fast pace. It scouts locations carefully, researching dozens of variables to predict where it can attract the most customers. For Enterprise, choosing new sites is a complex and costly science.

McDonnell piggybacks on his rival's efforts. He waits for Enterprise to pick a site—and then he tries to open a U-Save outlet as close as possible. Sometimes he'll set up shop right across the street. This makes U-Save's site selection a model of simplicity.

Military leaders can violate the principle of simplicity by assigning complex maneuvers to troops who lack the experience and expertise to follow through. You also need to avoid drowning your employees in too much unfamiliar information. If you give instructions that sail over someone's head, you've erred by expressing needlessly complicated points to someone who's ill-equipped to understand them.

This can happen when managers use industry lingo with new employees. One management consultant tells the story of a supermarket manager who told his employee to "go face the shelves." That sounds simple enough, but only if it's understood by everyone. In industry parlance, "facing" means pulling all products forward so that they're easier for shoppers to see as they wander down the aisle. Some time later, the consultant noticed the worker just standing in an aisle staring at the shelves.

Miscommunication doesn't just happen with new employees. Some years ago, a fatal airline crash occurred because of a miscommunication among a highly trained crew. Something unexpected happened just before landing. Cockpit voice recorders indicated that the captain called out, "Take off power!" He apparently meant for the copilot to advance the throttles to full takeoff power, but in the confusion of the moment the copilot understood him to say take the power all the way off. The copilot closed the throttles, and there was no time to recover from the error.

Aside from the dangers posed by industry jargon, it's also important to stick to essentials. When Burger King tried to launch a new, improved french fry in 1998, McDonald's executives insisted to their U.S. franchisees that the Golden Arches must win the fry war. McDonald's top brass told restaurant managers they were under a "full frontal assault" and had to "affirm our fries' superiority on the front lines" by staffing fry stations continually to monitor times and temperatures. As a result of this simple message, McDonald's managed to fight off Burger King's attack.

There is a tendency for some leaders to confuse the length of their remarks (whether written or verbal) with their importance. Yet brevity generally breeds simplicity.

Still, even the most concise communicators need to prepare clear directives. Ray Zeek, CEO of JD Steel Co. in Phoenix, rarely wastes words. Over the past 30 years as a commercial construction manager, he's made a conscious effort to embrace simplicity as a guiding principle of his relationship with employees.

"If employees can figure out any way to misunderstand you, they will," he says. "And it'll come back to haunt you." Zeek recalls a situation when he asked a supervisor to arrange for building materials to arrive at a construction site on a certain day. The supplies never showed up.

"That was a costly error of mine," Zeek says. "My mistake was to give overly complicated instructions. I gave too much information about what I wanted this person to do, instead of just boiling it down to the specific actions I needed him to take and that's it."

As a result of that incident many years ago, Zeek now applies a three-step process to communicate with simplicity:

1. **He prepares carefully** by numbering the key points he needs to express. This helps him rehearse his message and isolate the most essential steps he wants to get across.

2. **He discusses his points** with employees in a calm, unhurried tone. "I try not to rush into the room, talk and then rush out," he says. "I encourage questions and give-and-take. I like to express my directions verbally because I can expound on them a bit more if necessary."

3. **He follows up in writing,** providing a short, itemized to-do list.

Zeek's methodical approach shows that adopting the principle of simplicity involves thorough preparation. The time you invest in rehearsing your message can pay valuable dividends.

For example, when Carl Modecki took over as president of a large professional group—the National Association of Insurance Brokers—he composed a "15-second spiel" to remind his employees of their central mission: to represent large global insurance brokers around the world on federal, state and local issues and issues of common economic interest.

"That was a simple summary of what we did," Modecki says. "If I was talking with someone and I wanted to go into more depth, I could branch out from that statement to focus on educational issues or tax savings or other areas."

Executives with military training often appreciate the role of simplicity in business more than others do. "If there was one thing I learned in the Marine Corps, it was the value of clear communication," says Rod Walsh, owner of Blue Chip Inventory Service. "Marines cannot afford to miscommunicate because lives depend upon a clear understanding of the mission. Therefore, we were all asked to repeat our orders. This way, the person issuing the order will know if it has been truly understood."

Walsh applies this lesson to his business communication. "Ever since I began Blue Chip, I have asked my employees to repeat my instructions. Of course, I have to be diplomatic about it and will ask them in a roundabout way (such as 'If you were to repeat these instructions to Tom, what would you say?')."

Above all, the key to simplicity is to discipline yourself to limit your comments to what matters most. If you go off on tangents or lose your train of thought, it's harder for your audience to follow your instructions. If you get a sudden brainstorm, you may feel compelled to shift gears and toss in lots of ancillary information that would only muddy your core message.

Beware of overloading others with too much (or irrelevant) chatter. Isolate a single, compelling point and stick to it. Like a commander leading an attack, you can direct everyone's efforts most successfully by keeping your plans and words short and simple.

> ✔ **Executive Checklist**
>
> 1. Is the proposed plan the simplest one that will achieve the objective?
> 2. What are the key elements of the plan that must be conveyed?
> 3. What are the points most likely to be misunderstood?
> 4. Have I devoted sufficient time to planning how I will communicate my plan?
> 5. Do the plan's action and wording match the quantity and abilities of the resources available to execute the plan?
> 6. Can the plan be described to those involved in clear, unambiguous terms so they all know their roles and how each will contribute to achieving the objective?

Appendix

The 9 Principles of War

1. Objective

Direct all efforts toward a clearly defined, decisive, obtainable goal.

2. Offensive

Seize the initiative in a decisive manner, retain it and exploit it to accomplish your objective.

3. Mass

Concentrate your combat power at the decisive place and time.

4. Economy of Force

Allocate minimum essential combat power to secondary efforts.

5. Maneuver

Place the enemy in a disadvantageous position through the flexible use of combat power.

6. Unity of Command

For every objective, there should be unity of effort under one responsible commander.

7. Security

Never permit the enemy to acquire an unexpected advantage.

8. Surprise

Pounce on the enemy at a time or place and in a manner for which he's unprepared.

9. Simplicity

Prepare clear, easy-to-understand plans and clear, concise orders to ensure thorough understanding.

Executive Checklist

Use this checklist to evaluate your career or business plans in terms of the nine rules of war.

OBJECTIVE

1. Does my plan have one clear objective that, if met, will achieve the success I seek?
2. Is the objective attainable?
3. What conditions would trigger a re-evaluation of the objective?
4. Can I get "buy-in" for the objective from all necessary resources?

OFFENSIVE

1. Is my plan basically offensive in nature, seizing the initiative to control the fate of my career and my company's profitability?
2. What internal strengths or external weaknesses can I exploit by taking the offensive?
3. Exactly what offensive actions will I take?
4. How will the offensive actions I propose support my objective?
5. Do I have sufficient resources available to take these offensive actions?
6. Can I afford *not* to take offensive action?

MASS

1. What is the minimum level of resources required to achieve my objective?
2. Will my plan direct the maximum resources available at the time and place that will have the greatest impact on achieving my objective?
3. Am I making the best use of each resource at my disposal?

ECONOMY OF FORCE

1. Are all secondary objectives clearly focused on supporting the primary objective?
2. Are minimum resources devoted to the secondary objectives?

MANEUVER

1. Can I gather sufficient information about the competition to guide maneuvering?
2. Have I selected and organized resources with enough flexibility to change direction quickly and smoothly based on new information?
3. Are my people and I innovative enough to find and exploit competitor weaknesses as they appear?
4. Have I anticipated and planned for likely competitor responses?

UNITY OF COMMAND

1. Is only one person ultimately responsible for each mission I assign?
2. Is that individual informed and clearly up to the task?
3. Do all people taking part in the mission know who the single commander is and what their individual roles and authority will be?
4. Are effective two-way communications in place to pass information and directives in the heat of battle?

SECURITY

1. What potential threats (for example, competitor counterattacks, shifts in marketplace demands, regulatory changes) do I need to defend against?
2. Have I devoted adequate resources to defending against those threats?
3. Have I protected sensitive information from competitor access through monitoring or espionage?
4. Is it useful to sow misinformation to deceive competitors about my real intentions?
5. Do I have a contingency or fallback plan to follow should my offensive not go as planned?

SURPRISE

1. What opportunities do I have to surprise my competitors in the time, place or strength of my offensive?
2. Can I realistically achieve the element of surprise?
3. If I'm successful at achieving surprise, what actions will I take to capitalize on it?

SIMPLICITY

1. Is the proposed plan the simplest one that will achieve the objective?
2. What are the key elements of the plan that must be conveyed?
3. What are the points most likely to be misunderstood?
4. Have I devoted sufficient time to planning how I will communicate my plan?
5. Do the plan's action and wording match the quantity and abilities of the resources available to execute the plan?
6. Can the plan be described to those involved in clear, unambiguous terms so they all know their roles and how each will contribute to achieving the objective?